MW01074260

ÆROTOMANIA:

THE BOOK OF LUMENATIONS

Lavender Ink
New Orleans

Ærotomania: The Book of Lumenations
Adeena Karasick

Copyright © 2023 by Adeena Karasick and Diálogos Books.

Printed in the U.S.A.
First Printing

Cover art and interior graphics by the Author

Library of Congress Control Number: 2022949925
Karasick, Adeena
Ærotomania: The Book of Lumenations / Adeena Karasick;
p. cm.
ISBN: 978-1-956921-12-0 (pbk.)

Lavender Ink
New Orleans
lavenderink.org

ACKNOWLEDGMENTS

Thank you to the editors and publications where previous versions of this work have been published: *Live Mag!* #18, *Art and Poetry Journal*, NYC, 2021 (Jeffrey Cyphers Wright), *Paris Lit Up* (Gracie Bialecki and Matt Jones), *-X-Peri* (Daniel Y. Harris), *Silver Pinion* (d.c. wojciech) in both the online journal and the print anthology, *Silver Pinion: To Affirm The Marvelous*, Word Studio, Arizona, 2020; *Alligatorzine* 206 (Kurt Devrese and Heller Levinson), *Maintenant* 13: *A Journal of Contemporary Dada Writing and Art*, (Peter Carlaftes) Three Rooms Press, Paris, Spring, 2019; Boog City 15 Arts Festival Programme (David Kirschenbaum), *Good Weather for Media*, (Jane Ormerod, Thomas Fucaloro, David Lawton, George Wallace, Mary McLaughlin Slechta), New York, Jan. 2019; *Unlikely Stories* V. 20th Anniversary Issue. Ed. Jonathon Penton, New Orleans, 2018.

"House of the Rising S[o]ns" was translated into Italian and published in *Sciame / Swarm: Lestordite Cultural Association Anthology*, (Eds. Giorgia Monti and Serena Piccoli), Padova, Italy, Jan. 2019; *The Friendly Voice: The Secret Handshake*, Vol.3 Issue 11, (Michael Alzamora), Toronto, 2019, *Marsh Hawk Review*, (Daniel Morris), New York, Spring 2019, PerspectiveProject, ABC Avant-garde Bootcamp, (Sylvia Egger), Berlin, 2020; *Chant de la Sirène The Journal: Poetics and the Hybrid Arts* (Laura Hinton), Summer 2020, Fall 2022, *The Laurel Review* (Daniel Biegelson and Ariel Resnikoff), Winter 2022. Selections of the "Eicha" section have been translated by Runa Bandyopadhyay into Bengali.

Thank you also to the many airlines and images from Safety Cards, United Airlines (B777-200), Delta B7-900ER Safety Information, Delta E175 (00) Safety Information, American Airlines 737 10/19 Revision, American 737-800 05/18

Selections of Ærotomania, made into a video presentation: "Ærotomania: How the Airplane is Structured like a Language for the Womxn," Technology and Media Panel at the 21st Annual Media Ecology Association Convention, June 2020 available at https://youtu.be/lQTVOk8gFVM, and as a vispo videopoem created with Jim Andrews, music by Frank London: https://youtu.be/K0ANxhF6jTc.

Videopoems have been created for the "Book of Lumenations" section, in collaboration with Italian filmmaker, Igor Imhoff, with music by Frank London, (Eicha I also featuring vispo from Erogenous Zones by Jim Andrews and Daniel F. Bradley); exhibited in BeZine (ed. Michael Dickel, Israel, June 2021), at the Womxn, Language, & Technology Virtual Art Exhibit for the 22th Annual Media Ecology Convention: Dystopic Futures: Media Ecology in an Algorithm Society, Pontifical Catholic University of Rio de Janeiro, Brazil, July 2021; the Doctor Clip Roma Poetry Film Festival Edizione VIII, Rome, Italy, Dec. 2021 and at The 49th annual Louisville Conference on Literature & Culture since 1900, University of Louisville, Feb. 2022, and featured at Pratt University Libraries as part of the Artist Book Exhibition, Feb-April 2022.

Infinitely grateful to Avraham Abulafia, Walter Benjamin, Paul Celan, Jacques Derrida, Elliot Wolfson, Michael Wex, Ludwig Wittgenstein and Louis Zukofsky, whose loving traces shadowed throughout in an echography of desire; for the close readings and guidance through the various editions of this text: Maria Damon, bill bissett, Robert Kasher Z"L,

Marvin Davis for his continued and loving support, and for taking me to the South Hampton Shul on Tisha B'Av inspiring the *Eicha* piece; to Frank London for his endless inspiration and collaboration; and especially to Bill Lavender for his passionate focus and dedication to this text

Urgent and forbidding, brutal and internal, i thank too, each and every letter and the spaces between them from which these words emerge, where i forever hide you. And as these sentences of secret language rejoice around me growing in number—through the anguish and tumult, desolation and thirst, i have been comforted as they moisten my mouth, wet my tongue and forever keep me safe.

Against the decay and order, against life and against death,
against accident, constant threats from the radio, the newspaper
headlines all spreading the plague, against perfidy seeping down
from upstairs or up from downstairs, against a slow devouring
inside and being swallowed by the outside...
and with unprecedented endurance...
i sit, i wait, i smoke.

—Ingeborg Bachmann

THE BOOK OF LUMENATIONS

EICHA I

And as the city sits
in the ferocity of discordance
I will dwell alone in the fields

melting with provenance, tributaries
heredity.

The night is no confiture
in the dalliance of treacherous shade

stained in the moan of erasure.

And gone is the drifting splendor,
the veritas of naked signs' sacrifice
magnified in inconsolable deflection

Pass me in the hallways of your grid.

In the pandemonium of
my impress knit
in the livery of dwelling

Pass me, wretched
through the wounds of humiliation
curtseying in the
crush of knotted breakage, brackets

Weep me
in the pile-on of your policing.

For these are the amendments
the figura of chasms exiled in disinformation.

This is the lotted
my garden
corseted in collusion
herded platforms
domes of wilted bargaining
the picked ramparts of broken defense.

And this is the delegitimized.
vow's trauma blockages
in the grief-hardened hunger.

EICHA II

The theurgy of delight is a drawing down. The
urgency of the light is a
drowning dawn, the resurgence of the light is
adoring drawn; a
drawing down, a drowning dawn the
urgence, a drowning, a
dawning a knotted dawn the delight of the
light resurgent
alight in the urgent emergence; to light
in the days of our hunger
in the days of our hunger
emergence; to light

And in the ache of asylum

I have bent my bow
framed in the anchor of candied dalliance –

screaming in strung shadows, revenance

where limning sutures, festooned in sunshift

Lie with me
in the illicit quiver
of knotted conscience

Languish
through whispered harbors'
pressed exile
among evening's inheritance;

the providence of slipped

semes slants
sucking twilight
of latticed scatter

Lie with me
in our ash-starred silence

constellated

in the riveted drifts

And suck the sting of sun clung lettered-skin
as I open my mouth
wide against you; ink gnashed

in the twinned ignition of scar-studded scripts

And behold, the stretched vestige of sprayed hunger
whose singeing fingers devour

in the petulance of choked zones
slain in the scored synchrony of

slung slaughter

summoning as though it were a feast day
sprawled in the dandle

of the rippled signs
of chorused dawn

EICHA III

Sheltered in netted inlets
of ripped dyssemia, fleshy sequiturs, wisteria, the taste
of broken bans –

Hail the billow of campy siege, the truance
of gilded travaille

And make me dwell in the darkened wreckage
of feverish dread

In the censored resonance of pliant heaves;

The plated shudder of my parade.

Burn me in the binding bias in torqued harrow.

For I am woke in the swindled aperture of fibrous light;

And I am giddy with shaded want in the quiescence
of ludic clues

Naked with his yoke in my mouth

Let him sit sultry for he has laid upon me

Let him put his mouth into the dust

Offer his shackles to the smitten

Let him be filled with peaches

The load is my portion to those who wait;

Come to me --
in the undulance of unassailable labor

in the screaming revenance

Covet me
with re-sculpted signs
of foaming rupture

Make me come
in the refuse among the precipice

in the amnesty of affliction
rapt in the shadowed torrent

of hushed slaughter, peepholes Eyestreams

In the tell of the luring

And say: lick dawn.
In the frame of hushed lobbies

Suck solace in the eros of my city
And fine me in the engine of our demise

Cast your mask upon me

Water my flowing head -- and cut me
in the dripping petulance

of curled indices
in the call of farce

You have seen the ringing dalliance

seen the silty ode of fitful defiance

ground in the ferocity of mourning;

as you police me in the milk of daybreak

EICHA IV

As care curls / in her swirled whorl's
spurred leurre / stirred
spur of porous roar

whose flayed fray forêts
flurried fury fiery folly

flares in the florid lore
of soaring horror

in the ripped wrought
raw lot

And in the raging contagion
of the yoked hurrah
we are riddled in thick drift
and drunk with iniquity --

asking whose balletic thirst
is clasped
in the synonymy

of our yaysay, purer than sinew, and wet with dusk
ruddier than choral, sapphire, milking crimson syrups
sifted riffs of spilt surfeits

Whose skin a
buttered vortex of fruited
folds fluted affinities
of ripened whim

crowned in syllabic aberrance

as tongue-torqued sucked cleaves –

whose contours of thirsty flourish
lather in the inhabitants of
herded words?

And who frames the humming grafts
of grinding ligatures

whose prophecy pressed
in the witness of
blind stagger?

And through trysty cirques, censures
garmented in letters

who's calling out in the fingered folly

of lasooed swoonsay
through frisson, flares
slips, lapsed, mounting rapt

in the stop-watched sap scored arias
of purring rigor?

*

And whose ruched ramparts
mount in the
cradled bouquet

of whose drenched thresholds
of pursed favor
flutter in

whose fluted impasse
compassed in whose haunted walls
whose licked chambers
kissed in the porosity
of luxuriant exposure

*

anchored in slung sun-sucked spurs
succor's prurience
in the province of curled lure
whose chorused encore courts
as quilled squall coils
in scarred culled, queues, calling --

AS THE BAN PLAYS ON.

EICHA V

Our letters have been turned over to strangers
our light to aliens.

We have become orphans, our murmurs, widows.

Our nostalgia we have drunk for payment; our words come
by purchase.

And in the wracked circuits of asylum
we are arrested in the wrought of the wilderness.

Our skin is parched, scarred in the heat of hunger.

They have outraged whimsy in the cities.

Hegemony was hanged by its hands, curtained with
contingency

Hours carry the counting; mouths gagged under the policing

The prowl of our heart has ceased, our dancing
has turned to mourning.

Our skin has fallen.

Gone is the luster that lies longing through the shuttered
gates of sunwashed words

    girded
        skinside

through the
sprig of ripe
albeit.

Let the streets remember.
The rhythms and stairwells
remember, the costumed raucous
retching in the unbearable clearing
remember, Let the rooms remember, the stages and facades
let the mirrors remember the bus stations and bastions
shadows and fables. Let the grammar
of unfolding, of rotted speech
cracked caskets
cliffs, grifts, shafts, graphs
the torpor and swindles; let the skies remember

And carry the burden of our memory

in the picketed moor of loomed spool
lapsed apt porous spurred purr
parsed in the epoch / ellipse

i will worship language in the night,
lay violent hands on your marked cities.
i will clutch at lies; grow bestial in my dreams

                              slick with ripped script,
                    licking the funicular of jiggling
            particulars

will allow myself to be slaughtered like a beast.

                              *

And will worship –
as the would wooed
would you?
awed n the watered
wed
of
the
wander

widening

                              *

worship
through prurient piers pierced longing
bursts, bans, bridled signals --

worship
in the contiguous torrent
of huddled borders screaming
against your skin fortressed by
weeping thresholds' precipice.

So, pass through me in the folded fancy
of cracked madness

contoured in shivering silhouette's
wet arrêt /pirouette
of softened kisses' brackets
pastures, pulsing
sleepless through
scarred triggers

Pass through me fleeced
in the nonce / sensors of
fissured swarms

Through tongued torrents, tombs, settling ash
through the sift of symptoms' stalls whose wills wail
whorl in the weave of social flesh;
through tattered shadows margins dizzying wounds howls
spurs, spores, silence
cinders, blood as the walls bears down
weeping

through the hour of prismatic distortions
the hour of unease
the hour of secret chambers, errant temerity

shudders, silences, barricades
nursed in darkness

the hour of resplendent hunger
scandal, fumes, revulsion

the hour stretched in the horror
of un-nameable lament
of swollen words, windbent
and drunken --

the hour of our cunning

of cloistered torment shivering
in the hour of the hour

of re-scented prisons mouthed
in the fastened flaps
of flesh, breath
sirens, solace, prayer
labyrinths, shadows, ire --

the hour
of weighted garments, gussets, curtains
chasms // silent screams

wailing in the intimacy
of its alchemy

in the black and unyielding light
alight in our own shivering dream

Through light of fat language
The light of stretched testing, widening fear
The light of untidy probes which smell like

gags
thievery
acrobats
dancing bears

Pass through me
through the light of the light
of the distance screaming
in the nostalgia of the present

CODA:
When the Caesura Screams

In the eros of aching ethos
the caesura screams --

through cirque'elatory sequiturs, resistances
indices, ambient contingencies
skin sucked squalls, scalded
s'écrites, scandals, contours, entrées

in the fluttered tongue
of social shading

and screams through weaponized valences
shuttered in swung scripts, scores, crypts
clef[t]s, sirens, scrims

screams in the ache of clustered blood
lettered wounds, fingered
through the pressed lament of looped err's
eros limns limbs limbered *timbre*

as it maps our forward minced
through throbbing yields of raw rue wracked ague
in the aporia aria porous aura

of arced curves, curls, cœurs
clasps, lacs / unlocking the
clocked eros of lisped slips, slapped, tongue-teased
traced sweat, pressed precipice

of split tones re-tuned
in the grief of metered mutes

screaming in the improv
of illiberal ardor

Here, her
in mired err
whose scar
is clear

Hear her / here / whose heir
wears err's

shared prayer / where
care is rare

in
her
vey iz mir
tears shmear
where fear
is clear

as mirrored ire / error
where flared air
colored
in your care

TALMUDY BLUES II
For Michael Wex

Said the lexicon to the dialect:
Fecund idiom –

Sometimes this poem feels like it's
not the brightest candle in the menorah

that it was behind the door when the brains
were being given out

That it operates like a wise person
At night.

And even though
it's all pulped up and pressed with polemical discord
producing itself through performative memory and politics
establishing its own force and affect
of lived and embodied agency --

like a messy baba*meisse*

it's wearing its Talmudic lenses
waving its big *yicchus*

and groaning under the weight of its reference.

And though it's schlepping its mental furniture
sometimes it's doing *so not well*

feels like it's lying in the ground brokering
Babel hocking its china

sayin' some of these words are already
of blessed memory.

And, may all your truths fall out,
but one.

And may it ache fiercely.

This poem is a translingual
spliced, polysemic undead dybbuk

all transubstantiated with
highly transmittable accents and inflections
super-spreading its radical necessity
says it's *also* operating within
a zombie economy --

and is complicit in its own undoing.

And if you don't mind me saying so,
these letters look good for their age

all dressed up to be messed up,
are dropping their load
have a burden to bear
and all framboissey-faire / and schikered up
are getting their telos read.

And like no *shtuppeh* before the *chuppeh* --

says, don't eat it
before you read it.

For it is said,
sometimes the poem grows like an onion.
And sometimes I wish it a sweet death --

A truck filled with sugar should run over it.

'cause in these troubled times
this poem is shpritzin' like a *baschenbinder*

drowning in hard glovin'
and anti-semantic wipes

crying out
between Clorox and a hard place

sayin' Clorox me like a hurricane, Clorox lobster, Clorox my body til it hurts. Just Clorox a bye baby, Clorox the house, the Qasbah, i'm gonna Clorox with you, hoochie koo, Clorox, around the clock. Clorox til you drop, Clorox me all night long, (ama*deus*)! sweet little Clorox and roller. Just Clorox the night, Clorox me tonite, Clorox your heart out 'n put some viral grime in the jewbox baby –'cause i love Clorox and roll it's a Clorox 'n roll fantasy so Clorox me gently, crocodile Clorox and roll gonna save the world Long Live Clorox and Roll!

And like a "fake" Yiddishist in the *how's bayou [c]hut spa dicht!*
of gefiltered kerfuffle, all fa'mished in the ferkakta flourish of
all that's nu? moistish and varnished; **Hot gad ya!**

is reminding us --
that like the Maggid of Mezeritch
it's got a big *tisch*

And despite its strapped-on borsht-belted,
back-slashed skirts, swerves, slips
still doesn't have *what* to wear

and says --
Blessed be She, who dwells within the letters

For, sometimes the letters rule over her
and sometimes she rules over the letters
cleaving to the light of infinite possibility

But it won't buy you common sense.

As i always say, the letter is matter which moves matter

And in the wander of our discontent

HOUSE OF THE RISING SON[S]

Whipcord. Pushback. Glass House.
Bleak House, crack$_{ed}$ House
detached T House, covefy House, tap House, trap House –
in the House where Nobodaddy lives
The call is coming from inside the House

of flickering facts
This House of wax

of curtains, cages. Cacausuckers. Unaccountably
curled, coded, coiled / The King
is in his counting House
Divided *in da House* of flying daggers
in the House of 1000 corpses.

This IS the legend of Hell House this monster
House of dead rats, black bread
eins tzvei drei fear House of horror, haunting
by the edge of the Leak.

Sick House, Gold House, Card House, Kill House

of props, prank, mirrors
shadows, shutters, trauma, triggers, troll House
bone House, shellshocked, blow House
of nightmares; vacancies, surfaces and dread.

House of skin, sinking
slaughterhouse, snake House

torture-House; dead House, damned House
lopsided country House.

The crooked House twinkling
in the moonlit supremacies
in the violence of paranoiac torque

No safe House, funhouse, lighthouse, party House
papered with shade –

House of 1000 candles. A playhouse
with laughing windows.
that drips blood, terror, hubris
Acid House of fools. Red House
of mad souls.

Who *is* the Master of this House
of madness, of sand, of fog
on the edge of the galaxy
with no view of the *see*

Big House, hothouse, house-broken stash House
whowhatwhen*where* hows
of intolerance. That screams / emoluments
through beckoning, (w)reckoning, ripped roarin, rathaus
ICE house, spliced House, jurymandered swine House,
not a *very,very,very, fine House*, but as you huff, n puff
'n blow your House [ ], "cleaning" the House, Iraquin'
the House -- a plague on both our [ ]

i'm still betting on the House.

CHECKING IN II

Fake News is at the Pho Bar

Mister Good Bar thinks this is fubar

Thin Lizzy's watching her carbs

The smoker, the joker and the mid-night toker
are wanting a vape

Old Man Beaver is wanting a 5 cent cigar

The pedagogue is in the synagogue

The luddite is going analog

Microsoft is getting hard

Form is wet with Content's Dream

Deleuze and Guattari are eating 1000 Platinos

Th'Oaten Flautist is eating Flautus

Chiaroscuros are at the Churrascaria

Chick Corea is at the Tequileria

Siouxie is eating sashimi

Aer Lingus is serving vaniglia

Longinus is getting wet

Christina Rosetti likes this

And says pluck it and suck it "pit it pit it little saddle pear say"

Per Se says it's all heresay

Binaries are doubling down

Hulsenbeck's having Malbec

Saussure's sipping Sancerre

Comic Sans is doing without

The 12 Tribes are at BamidBar

Sacher-Masoch is *serving* it

Hugo Ball's having highballs

The Rebbe of Babli is sipping Bubbly

Erving Goffman is quaffin' it

Korzybski's sippin' it

Havelock's unlockin' it

Harold Innis is swiggin' Guinness

McLuhan's all Macallan®

Jacques Elul is drinking alcool

UBERmensch's drinking Cab

Starry Night is lit

Petit Fours are at the Betty Ford

3rd Party Cookies are getting some candy

Overdots are ascending on high

Bold Italics are refusing to move into an upright position

The plums that were in the icebox are getting juiced

Small Batch Bourbon is in a Tiny House

Walt Whitman is enjoying some summer grass

Thelonious Monk is smokin' skunk

Johann Gottfried von Herder is hoarding it

Plato is opening his Pharmacy

Yahoo! is opening some Happy Tabs

Roman Jakobson is getting diaChronic

Jack is getting all cranked up

Hansel and Gretel are getting baked

Brion Gysin is cutting it up

Jack the Ripper ♥ this

Hot Media is unzipping itself

Emily Dickinson is going into the fog

Hello Kitty is grabbing her pussy

The Wandering Jew has lost herself

Anubis is smoking Cannabis

The Princess's got Lephroaig in her throat

Flogging Molly is eating a Tamale

Flat Foot Floogie is doing the rhumboogie

Ob la di is saying oh-blood-ugh!

Obadiah is saying La-Di-Da

Paul Valéry is saying Valer ahahahahahaha!

Raw Data Has Been Stripped Bare by her Bachelors

The Long, Long Sleeper is Woke

Abandoned Airbnb's in Araby

John Ashbery is where black swansdown settles on the city

William Butler Yeats is where the Inn is free

Yes Man is in the Noosphere

Arthur Rimbaud is at the Four Seasons in Hell

Geppetto is in a ghetto

Frodo is in a grotto

The cäiman is in the Caymens

The Layman is saying Amen

Google is mapping the territory

The World Wide Web is at The W

Virginia Woolf has a Zoom of one's own

Narcissus is pinning himself

Tormented polyglots of sensorium are sharing their screen

Edvard Munch is sharing his Scream

Doctor Moreau is at the pyramids of Meroe

Joan Miró is drinking Merlot

The Pied Noir are drinking Pinot Noir

The Cocteau Twins are at the Double Tree

The proletariat are at the Marriot

Citizens in lockdown are using Homeric language

Helvetica Ultra Light is using its indoor voice

cOvid is metamorphosizing

Idioms are being contaminated

Fellini's having quarantinis

van Gogh's got gin and mango

Frances Ponge's nursing a mélange

L'chanteuse is having chartreuse

The sine qua non is overflowing

bpNichol is sinking in sin's kin

Lynyrd Skynyrd is in the skin i live in

Fats Waller is with Iceberg Slim

525,600 minutes are at Midnight Moment

The Sixty Minute Man is reading The Book of Hours

Minute Maid is taking minutes

Time is on your side

Kronos got Corona

Copper and aluminum are exposing their inner mettle

Dirty Concretists are overwriting

Gaudy Heavy Face is WRIT LARGE

Robust hegemonics & Spanx© are re-shaping identity

Subjectivists are saying, there's "no [O]there there"

Non-essentialists are singing, "there's no *isness* like show *isnesss*, no *isness* i know"

The system is closed

The Lady's Yes is cautiously optimistic

The House of Pancakes is waffling

The Flexitarian is having a healthy dialogue

Heidegger's just looking for some Authenticity

Immanuel Kant is saying, "i simply can't"

Conjunctions are negotiating an erotics of the between

Triads are having a 3-way

Polyphonic translations are semantically triangulating

The cold relentless vest is craving a coat of arms

The Boogaloo's making a hullaballoo

Edamame is with Nobodaddy

The Weird Sisters are establishing their own hagiography

The Ayin Hara is eyeballing it

Noah's sheltering in his Ark

Arced discourse is watching its Spread

The Cosmic Chef is reading a Tale of Two Zitis

Chef Boyardee is reading the Rime of the Ancient Marinara

John the Baptist is at Chopt

Le Chat Noir is at Château Noir

Idioms are out on Parole

The ampersand is with the analysand

George Sand is saying *Santé, L'chaim, Nostrovia*

Proust is saying *Prost!* Remembering his drinks past

Loose ends are at the side bar

Footnotes are toe-ing the line

Underscores just wanna experience the *subline*

Zoomers are feeling boxed in

The half-full cup says emptiness is endless

Copulas are beside themselves

Commas are giving pause

Entropic worlds are folding inward

Filler words are lost in the *Umvelt*

Marinetti and Ferlinghetti are with their Olivetti

Aleatory is telling another story

The Jewish Giant is overcome with unintentional greatness

The lone weaver is reading pattern recognition

The shmata is fighting against its own pRAGmaticism

Cursors are creating their own precursors
singing, "Ring around the eros-ey, apocryphalic poesie"

The center is losing its balance

Hot medium is shpritzing

Spit Temple is gobsmacked

The drizzle of the dying day is watching its droplets

Thunder is pointing to the technological rumble
of social change

Messages are hiding their mediums

Yahweh is using Huawei

Damascus is unmasking

Apprisers are uprising

Protesters are pro-testing

Minota(u)rians are negotiating a labyrinthine r/evolution

Revolutionaries are chanting, "support our tropes"

The Maggid of Chernobyl is seeing the light

Reb Menachem Nachum is singing, "The BeShT
is yet to come"

Sumerians are singing, "I love a [language] in cuneiform!"

Lacan likes language in a lacunae form

Mashiach is withholding his big reveal

Media Ecologists are doing t.v.ological analyses

Skeptics are negotiating all the ins and doubts

Hotel.com's negotiating all the inns and routes

Schipol's gettin' a Sky Pool

Synechdoche's in Schenectady

Arachne's in an infected Quay

Paul Celan's at the salon

Omicron's in Milan, sayin, *t-t-t-t-t-ouch me
I wanna be diiiiirty*

Activist margins are left justified

New systemic models are re-posing

Deepfakes are drowning in shallow discourse

Vexed lexis is regulating access

Xerxes is xeroxing

The immunocompromised are still Cloroxing

Sad Boy's Sad Boy is playing with his enWii

Kant is looking for Duty Free

Lexicons are flyin'

Dangling modifiers are going off the derech

Square Roots are being radicalized

Potentia is plotting

Potus is plotzing

Postcard Poems and Prisons are reducing their sentences

Definitions are still in lockdown

Charles Sanders Peirce is lookin' for change

Close readers and Active Listeners are saying, we're all in this together

ÆROTOMANIA

"The Airplane is an extension of the entire body" (Marshall McLuhan, *Extensions of Man*)

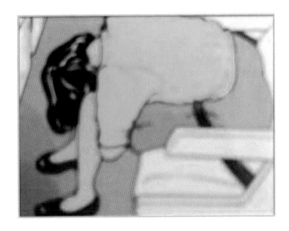

Fasten your strap
&
prepare for takeoff

In the partition of skin wrapped like paper like prayer through the echoes of hushed walls؛ welling through chambers of night؛ between leisure؛ labor؛ utility and pleasure؛ the airplane as an erotic theater؛ a social text of secret motives؛ functions like a language ...

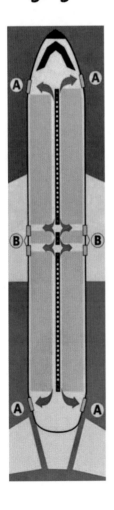

a hyperculture of forces and relations؛ chains of connections؛ affections insurrections؛ systems cycles؛ patterns and dispersions in an aerotic ecology of sovereignty and sacrifice

We are the letters travelling through space.
Seated letters speaking ourselves
against the sky inverted through flying circuits
coded ciphers secrets' shaded silence
of shuttered truance

We are the letters,
the interletters between rows of text
awake / in the flux of discomfiture

The spoken sentence
between destinations
of dissemblance
liaised in the labor of
hours aisles eros sorrows aeros

parataxiing down the runway

in the heft of day --

The airplane is structured like a language

And we are the letters reassembling
in a shifting ensemble;
illicit and clandestine sequestered in the curved body
of arced crevices, potence, platforms, portals,
promise

we are the floating signifiers
flying through a body of conventions
volatile and unspooled, looping

*According to the Digital Equipment Corporation'
in many aircraft, the rightmost seats have letter
designations HJK, skipping the letter I*

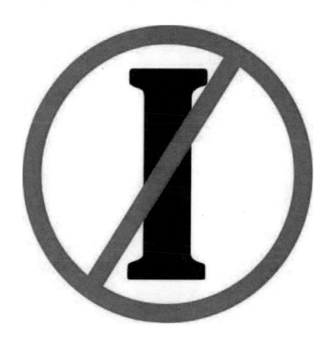

as mathematically speaking,

a PLANE is a point a line

and a two dimensional space

.i.i.i.i.i.i.i.i.i.i.i.i.i.i.i.i.i.i.i.i.i.i.i.i.i.

Inscribing itself as a site of radical intersubjectivity
through an ærosdynamics of radiant space

the very body of the airplane highlights subjectivity
as a spectrum of differential r/elations

and we are flying

through intersectional veils, chariots,
heavens and throne rooms
plays, plaise, palaces, seals and ascents
through the waters of high walls
and the halls of the unseen

**highlighting how like in Heidegger's formulation,
the same is an endlessly repeatable identity**

AA BB ABAB

**held together in radical dissimilarity, irreducibly bonded
in their (dis)union [2] --**

**further extended in McLuhan's 1948
antidialectical tetradic axiology of metaphor and analogy[3]**

A is to B so C is to D

AB:CD

As attested in the Sefer Yetzirah (*Book of Formation*),
in accordance with midrashic and talmudic exegesis,

the world was created through the combination of letters

Each substitution and transposition
of the letters condenses light
into a life force, made by forming, weighing,
combining and transforming the letters

resulting in 231 combinations
reconfigured into groups of 3 and 4 letters

A B C	D E F G	H J K	ROW 8
▢▢▢	▢▢▢▢	▢▢▢	ROW 9
▢▢▢	▢▢▢▢	▢▢▢	ROW 10

Each lettered combination is understood as a gate and through these "gates" creative power goes out into the universe. The 231 gates are created by pairing each of the letters of the alphabet with one another until all 231 letters combination are formed.

How to combine, weigh, and exchange them?

A with all and all with A; B with all and all with B;

G with all and all with G; and all of them turned around

going forth through two hundred and thirty one gates,

And the whole creation and all meaning proceed

From letter combination[4]

gates of connection
    annexion, synnexion

                       gates of entry
                  gates of desire

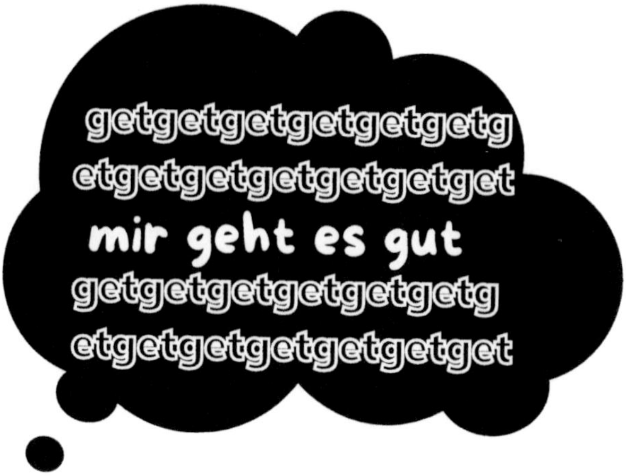

getgetgetgetgetgetg
etgetgetgetgetgetget
mir geht es gut
getgetgetgetgetgetg
etgetgetgetgetgetget

**Q Gate, R Gate, S Gate
T Gate, U Gate**

wie gehts?

"gates of the imagination,
gates as the imagination"

FOR JEWS CELEBRATING THE DAYS OF AWE GATES REFER TO ONE'S FUTURE BEING SEALED IN THE BOOK OF LIFE

closing of the gates, yet opening into new
passages, sentences, scrolls, arcs, lines of flight

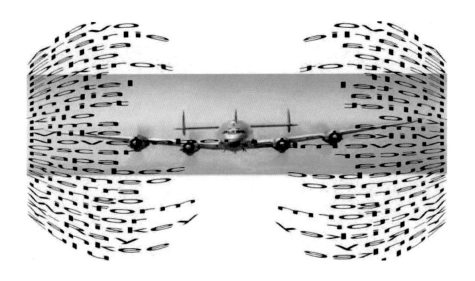

constellated in the abecedaries
of the abyss [6]

& says fly me by night to the
river [de]river over the rainbow
fly me faster than angels so fly
as the sky flying without wings
as sparks fly enfleurage i was
born to fly so fly with me
through the flux of form through
refueled folly volleyed veils
voiles volér réveillé all luminous
voluminous flee flyten' fly flug
me by the seat of your pense fly
me like a butterfly fly as
flamingos flyin the coupe fly
free and fly blind buttressed
from the inside like a flying f*ck
on the fly to the moon over the
dateline as the sky flies awake

We are the letters traveling through space
through planes of *Boeing* in time,
whose costume, custom, décor
decorum of patterned mazes, fathoms, pixels,
flickering through tumult

masked and breathing
reclining or upright

we are the letters
unraveling though space

That space where language circulates

According to Merkabah mysticism, exotic angelic beings with awesome strength and powerful flying wings served as heavenly tour guides carrying creative energy through the celestial spheres. As it is said, the chariot flew Elijah from earthly dimensions to heavenly ones in a great burst of light and speed

The world record for height by an air-breathing aircraft is 85,135 ft, set in an SR-71 Blackbird in 1976. Most US military aircraft can exceed 50,000 and most commercial jetliners cruise somewhere between 30,000 and 45,000 feet above mean sea level. The X-15 have flown higher but are classified as rockets, because they carry their own source of oxygen, instead of using the air. As aircraft climb to higher altitudes, the air outside gets thinner, therefore modern commercial jets compromise and are pressurized to an altitude of 5000-8000ft. A typical commercial jet cruises at 28-35,000ft (up to 6.6 miles of altitude), with the exception of the Concorde designed to fly at 45,000 ft. Although many jets could fly at higher altitudes, they are usually certified to an altitude in regards to safety. The new generation Boeing 737 is certified to 41,000 ft (7.8 miles). The current versions of the famous U2 military spy plane, originally designed in the 1950s can cruise at up to 90,000 ft (17 miles), while The Stealth Bomber cruises at up to 50,000 ft (8.3 miles) with increasingly higher cruising altitudes

Opening to higher and higher levels
so high in the night sky

the airplane appears as a spark of light

A flash in the darkness
and from this most infinitesimal point
of concentration, contains
all the future within it

or as in Heidegger's translation of
Heraclitus preserved by Hippolytus,
the flash of lightening that surrounds
the presencing of all things

present while itself remaining
concealed from being present
"not as presence presently absent
or an absence absently present

but as the absent present
that continually withdraws in the spectacle

of its present absence" [8]

And like the flash of primordial letters
clothed in the nothingness of being
enshrouded in the disquiet
of dissembling –

letters, like desire itself, "that ran and returned
across the face of the heavens," the airplane embodies
all that is to come; comes and keeps coming

avionaveniravionavenir

in an ever-arriving future.[9]

For the very shape of the airplane is reminiscent of the letter Alef,[10] the first letter of the Hebrew alphabet.

Symbol of infinite and contemporaneous beginnings –
it's constructed from two Yods, one above and one below
with a diagonal line, between them
representing the higher world and the lower world
separating and connecting the two

And through chambers of light
rungs of life
ærotically connecting
upper and lower worlds

all brimming with interior struggle and yearning
hiddenness and longing --

Aloft in our throne-seats, we are flying
through celestial vows, vaults, voids,
cavities, caves, caveats
flying / with anguished abandon

ravished, moaning and pinned
against the unwieldy sky
undressing before us

gathering clouds
of data / wisped ripples
systems, rhythms
as skies' signs swerve serving

caressed by nonsemantic ciphers

the airplane performs the Kabbalistic secret of the "white letters." For, according to the teaching of late 18th C. and early 19th C. Hasidic master, R. Isaac of Berditchev, disciple of R. Dov Baer of Mezeritch, the Great Magid,

not only do the black

signs constitute letters

but the white spaces

that encompass them

Clothed in invisible white letters --

cirrocumulus. cirris.
stratus. altocumulus. nimbostratus. stratocumulous.
altostratus. cirrostratus. lenticular. noctilucent.
cumulonimbus.   cumulus.   collusive.

the airplane stands in for all that is invisible,
visible, risable, li[a]sable
entwined in each other
and as black light drenched in white light
pressed against
purring torment as
lettered sweat seeps through
muffled shouts, splits, rips
rocketing darkness
as the night squats
strapped against the sky

moving through and across
geo-political, socio-ethnic and gendered borders

amassing memory, data
enacting a multicultural polyvalent poetics of
inclusion -

asserting itself not so much as a bourgeois interior
of imperial space, but one of shifting hierarchies,
conventions, investment.

The airplane is flying like a language

a distributional force gliding
between local and global figurations

fluxuries, luxuries, liaised
within the dialogics of recirculation

reproducing meaning through robust routes

> *airplane's root from 19th C.*
> *French aéro- 'air' + Greek -planos 'wandering',*
> *So, through an ærotically inscribed*
> *intralingual historicity*
> *the airplane is literally wandering like a language*
> *inscribed in differal, deferral*

or re-rooting

> *In contemporary French, en plein*
> *literally means*
> *'in the middle'. Thus, inscribed*
> *in its very name, the plane is*
> *always en medias, en route*

reminding us
how like language's cultural identification
and aesthetic properties
the airplane, occupies an in-between space,
a non-place, s'passez;

between arms, rests, thighs,
fingers dripping flesh ---

pursed, pressed, porous and en proces --

And all nomadic and vagrant
like the airplane

sometimes language gets hijacked
　　through foreign bodies, elements of otherness
　　dyssemically re-routed through de-familiar zones

sometimes languages collide

sometimes it is subject to layovers

And sometimes,

as anagrammatically, *airplane* can be read as *real pain*

its slippery body, of multiple entrances,
moist gaps, apertures[11]

is just longing for some turbulence

With palimpsestic, decentered desire
and propelled by thrust

the airplane, as language, enters as a body
navigating curves, corridors,
windy torment, raiment, hunger –

through syllabic gasps
propulsive rasps naked aching
as the sky opens

consenting sky

ink-drenched and garmented
with specters, slippage, rafts, corridors, constellations

taste its vocabulary, it says

through star-studded galaxies

(((galexis)))

axes of incidence, prospects

Reminding you:
the closest excess might be behind you

> *Re-rooted, from Old French plein;*
> *from the Latin plenus; the proto-Italic, plenos;*
> *proto-Indo-European plhonos; plainly said,*
> *the airplane refers to that which is plenty,*
> *pregnant, excessive, full* [12]

REFUSELAGE

Thus, inscribed in its very name,
the plane embodies a double bind of excess and lack
all that is material and ethereal, illusive and policed -

a glossopoeisis of sublime vistas
yet also restriction, regulation

NO SMOKING NO TOOTHPASTE NO FIREARMS NO LIGHTERS
NO SMALL TOOLS NO LIQUIDS NO GELS NO AEROSOLS NO
LIGHTERS NO MATCHES NO BATTERIES NO GEL INSERTS NO
WRAPPED PRESENTS NO BOX CUTTERS NO ICE AXES PICKS NO
KNIVES NO MEAT CLEAVERS NO RAZOR-TYPE BLADES NO
SCISSORS NO HOCKEY STICKS NO MACE NO PEPPER SPRAY NO
BRASS KNUCKLES NO BILLY CLUBS OR BLACK JACKS NO
AMMUNITION OR FIREARMS NO BB GUNS COMPRESSED-AIR
GUNS NO PELLET GUNS STARTER PISTOLS NO FIREWORKS OR
FLARES NO BLASTING CAPS DYNAMITE NO FUELS OR
GASOLINE LIGHTER FLUID OR FLAMMABLE PAINTS NO
TURPENTINE BLEACH PAINT THINNERS REPLICAS OF
INCENDIARIES NO CHLORINE OR HOVERBOARDS NO STUN
GUNS NO SPRAY PAINT NO VAPES NO DRONES NO TEAR GAS

And just like how weaponry, explosives and other
contraband materials regularly slip through security
system undetected,[13] similarly, within the complex
folds of text, explosively transgressive "dangerous
materials" are often smuggled in and hidden,
resulting in revolutionary and renegade thinking

where the sky's the limit

through a spoken web
of ribboned space

countersigned through a choral orchestra
of quiet violence, pulsing
rubrics, lacunae

For, according to Lacan, it is in the relation to this limit,
crossing the threshold of this limit,
where ultimate pleasure resides[14]

and says:
Touch anywhere to begin
or press « Enter »

As an elaborate site of limits, em/braces, pat-downs,
buckles, straps, masks,
the airplane establishes itself as a polyamorous
space of fetishistic excess.

And through a libidinally vertiginous, erotic mirroring
of tops, bottoms, bodies and belongings
blurred between seeing and being seen, seeing into;
touching and being touched
in public space

we are the seated letters fastened to each other
strapped down and writhing, mewling, bucking,
like feral lionesses
growling and scratching and biting [15]

subordinated and taking command
through restrictions, constrictions
paths of torment

we are the seated letters with our masks beneath
us, bound by safe words, modes, modules, devices,
desire and consent

and through private turbulence

metal clasps, belts, grips, plugs, pedals,
gangways, rudderball, yokes, joysticks,
plied light, fingers, gaspers

thick with shade

we are "in harmony with our [prospective] annihilation"[16]

& asks you to please put on your masque before débording[17]

And as we rub shoulders
with abundance

between what is seen and unseen; heard
between scenes, screens, schemes, screams
cockpits, lifts, radios, buds

as both a site of public and private space,
the airplane celebrates itself
as an ever-shifting site of escape and refuge

reminding us how escape
is always entry into new dimensions –

This is particularly underscored in the fact that
the gematria for the Hebrew word for airplane,
"matos" also relates to the word for
captive (ASSIR) and to flee (ARAH)[18]

SO NOT ONLY AT THE NEXUS
OF ESCAPE AND REFUGE BUT
OF CONCEALMENT
AND EXPOSURE

ALL SERVILE, SURVEILLED
A SALIENT VALENCE
OF SECRETS SWERVES VEILS

THE AIRPLANE FUNCTIONS
AS A FOUCAULDIAN
PANOPTICON

with a concerted distribution
of bodies, lights, gazes

a privileged place

where one is "able to judge at a glance
without anything being concealed from [it]
how the entire establishment is functioning"[19]

AND WITH THE GAZE ALERT EVERYWHERE
WE ARE FLYING
THROUGH MICROPOLITICAL
EVASIONS COMPLICITIES AND REFUSALS
FLYING
WITH MILITANT AND
TRANSFORMATIVE RESISTANCE
THROUGH TIGHT
SPACES
AND HARD ARCHITECTURE
BLACK
BOXES
AND
ERASURE PRISONS
MISPRISIONS
POWER AND
VISIBILITY THROUGH
DECENTERED AISLES
SYSTEMS APPROACHES DISSENT

RE-PRODUCING AND
REFIGURING WAYS OF SEEING

seatbuckled. in. contained. resistance.

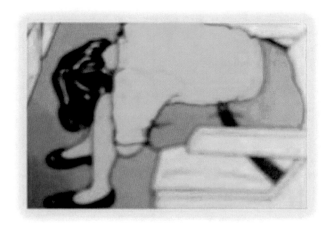

And through an aerobatics of shock cord,
coils, kisses, harnesses, gusty thrust-face
ferrule flange fingered crankshaft
of hood valve honeycombed coulomb,
monocoqued cockpit, yaw --

the airplane, as language[20]
is marked by uncertain subjects

all vulnerable and aporetic
and in constant negotiation

through contemporaneous constellations
consultations, councils, consoles, kinships

operating as a democratic space;
a dialectics of otherness, grounded
in ex-static possibilities

NOT JUST AN AIRPLANE BUT A THEIR PLANE

punctuating the sky ornamented
with jeweled light, circumcised words
folding into and across dripping abscissas,
aluminous surfaces
marking covenant, between all that is overt, covert,
coveting ravenous, cavernous
in parasidical polysemia

disseminatively slicing
as the plane cuts sky cuts skin cuts off, into
rites of passage

flying through embroidered curtains
robed in metallic spans
veiled weft, woven breath

of gilded spurs all slippery and lexuriant –
through laws, lulls layers,
orbits, ambits, gambits
gaming the sky

The *Airplane Game* or *Plane Game* is a style of pyramid scheme active in the 1980's which involved joining an "airplane" where "passengers", "flight attendants" and "co-pilots" payed pilots who collected $12,000 from passengers to retire. The game progressed until each participant became "a pilot" who then themselves collected $12,000. Though the common version required passengers to pay $1,500 to receive $12,000 as a pilot, some airplanes were being run with $5,000 passengers and a $40,000 pilot payout.

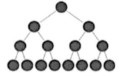

Also called Concorde, Golden Galaxy,
Cosmic Adventure and Flying Starship
the airplane remains a site of games plots, schemes

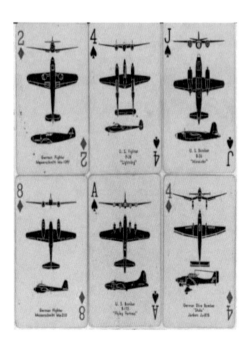

Highlighting Wittgensteinian language-games and Lyotardian Game Theory, where even if we know the codes of "the game," the rules are always-already local, fluid, changing and contested, the airplane reminds us how, with every enunciation, re-articulation, there is a celebration of discourse as a series of traces markings and echoes

phantomatic projections, introjection,
exilic trajection;

a *syllaboration* of communication as polysemous play

where we inhabit, dwell
in the interstices, the aporias in a superfluity of folds
in the *unheimlich* space of multiplicitous systems
of social and cultural signification

a hybridized syncretic space between cultures and idioms
where that interlingual complexity
doesn't *close down* but builds dialogue

and celebrates the deterritorialization
of *joue le jeu* the *en jeu*; of *appelez's* play
of seduction addiction s'diction of slippery ellipses,
where play's placed in a *plaisir* of pliant pleas
a replayed display, where "the play's the thing"

like language itself, marked by distances
values, solitudes, convergences

the airplane travels through compressible fluid mediums
of elastic particles
aching and desirous

in conversation with the sky

where thinking comes alive in dialogue, through
modes of engagement, rejoinders[21], establishing a
collaborative poesis that averts a single lyric
destination but rather deploys multiple psyches,
engines, economies, conversing reversals, subversals

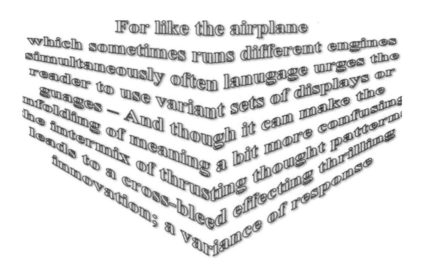

For like the airplane
which sometimes runs different engines
simultaneously often lanugage urges the
reader to use variant sets of displays or
guages – And though it can make the
nfolding of meaning a bit more confusing
he intermix of thrusting thought patterns
leads to a cross-bleed effecting thrilling
innovation; a variance of response

effecting a diasporic polyvalence / polyVOLÉnce
negotiating itself

as an uncanny object

a systemic node in bracketed space.

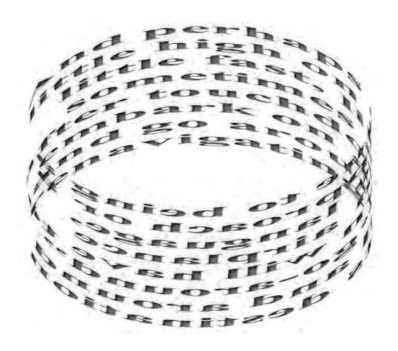

And like how for Derrida, *il n'y a pas de hors-texte* or for Poe or McLuhan, the fish is never separate from the water, the pilot is never separate from the palette. As such, the poet as both pilot and pilot project, provides a blueprint for further exploration, application, experimentation, extrapolation, exportation, complication, elevation, elation becomes

a   pilot   light

an   ignition

source --

for more

powerful

& incandescent

illumination

ærotically spreading its wings
flashing[22] you before takeoff
waiving its well-formed upturned tail[23] (tale)

with wide-bodied elegance
each model struts along the runway --

Delta
Haus
of Asiana
Serbia
Avianca
Haus of Emirates
Pegasus Namibia
TigerWing Sunwing Haus of Vistara Volaris Porter Peach Mango
Haus of Kulula of Vueling Silkair Luxair Aer Lingus, Volotea Aeroflot, Haus of Spirit Spring
Swoop Aerolineas Jeju Jet2 JetBlue Fiji Finnair FyBe French bee Frontier Virgin
Country TAP Pegasus
Skylanes Scoot
SAS Haus of
Tran-sat
Vistara
Saudi

And through sculpted inscriptions, encryptions
permission, emission, admission, transgression

hiding in plane cite

sometimes it's crying out under the weight of its
reference

re-navigating

from one destination
to another

performing its own genealogy

A desiring machine[24]
which functions smoothly at times
at other times in fits and starts

la machine de l'éte, machine of being

marked by its big nose and full body
gliding through an ærotics of visceral clusters,
syllabic grafts, lifts, rifts, drifts: a chordal accordance
of discordant concordance

a flight of fancy
a Concord[25] of *s'ecrit* sounds

exploding through improvisatory rituals, customs
cartographically re-grafting itself
in the degralescence of its own vagrancy

all exilic, textilic, diasporic and nomadic
asserting,

So much dépense[26]
upon

a red steel
aero

g'liazed with rain
water

beside the flight
check ins

And just like how truth in language
is never naked and exposed

as nakedness is another form of apparel
an unmasking that is masking the mask,
the unveiling that is veiling the veil --

with her long arms hugging the sky,
the naked body of the airplane is "garmentless"
semantically ascending through the
utterance of its being

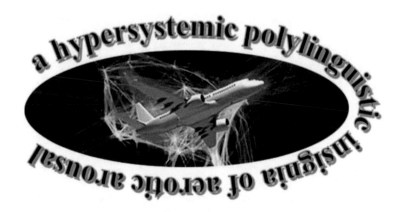

a hypersystemic polylinguistic insignia of aerotic arousal

Yet maintaining its flight path,
it mirrors the functioning of syntax;
the set of rules, principles and processes that
govern the structure of sentences in a given language.
Defined by semantic corridors
conventions, altitude blocks
fixed coordinates

both the airplane and language operate
within rigorously calibrated socio-linguistic,
technologic and geographic systems highlighting
how limit and restriction engender ultimate possibility[27]

واستخدام الصافرة لجذب الانتباه.

This sense of paradox is further evident
in that both the airplane and language

are the "home" that is the place of isolation
and aloneness but also the place of unison,[28]
the haven of solitude and the womb of relationality

**soaring through networks
transfers avowals consonance
aeros eros contours corridors
recourse concourse en cœur's
discourse; trails tracks
lines queues**

QAnon and on / They just keep on trying...
QAnon and on, On and on,
QAnonn and on

and with giddy truance, says: s Q's me or --
skip the queue

cruising through a circuitry of skewed cues --

we are the letters traveling through space and time
private and public, intimate and open

as par avion – where secreted in its very name,
l'envois,[29] envoy (messenger) carrying la vois (to see)
and voi[x] (to voice) and by extension *voile* (veiling)

And through the reveille veils, avails, values, volés
as secrets mist binding days where dawn threads
majestically through the raging sky

the airplane reminds us that between
seeing and saying
and the infinite veiling and unveiling
of language, meaning, being,
communication and travel

as medium, *en medias*, as message and messenger
it's always already massaging the ærotics
of the secret and the social
through an ever-swirling circulation
of permission, submission
gradation, celebration

measured and weighed

encasing the weight of jouissance the weight of reference
representation the weight of context contrails
contingency, control the weight of expectation,
translation, relation, topographies, echographies
the weight of seduction, memory and
upheaval the weight of meaning's
production and the
price of process

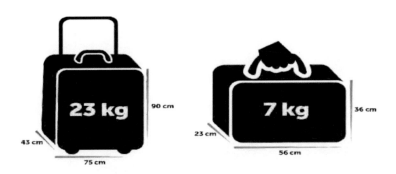

claimed and reclaimed from an ever-spiraling carousel[30]

reminding us

that the limits of [our] language

means the limits of [our] world

(Wittgenstein)

Thank you for flying with us. Please enjoy a safe and easy transition to your final destination.

1. According to the DEC, the letters, I, O, Q, S, or Z must be avoided. The remaining letters are called the DEC alphabet.

Occasionally, aircraft with a seating structure of 2+2 may letter the seats as "ACDF" to keep with the standard of A/F being window and C/D being aisle on short-haul aircraft (which generally have 3+3 seats). If the economy cabin is ten across, labeled ABC-DEFG-HJK, the Business Class cabin is often labeled AC-DG-HK for a six across layout, with A-DG-K for a four across First Class. A notable exception is Delta Air Lines, who uses sequential letters regardless of cabin layout on all aircraft (AB-CD-EF in Business Class and ABC-DEF-GHJ in Economy).

Some airlines omit the row number 13, reputedly because of a widespread superstition that the number is unlucky. This is the case with Lufthansa, for example (as shown on the Lufthansa A321/100 seating plan). Emirates used to have a row 13, but on their latest A380 aircraft have removed it (as shown on Emirates A380-800 seating plan). British Airways is less superstitious.

2. Heidegger, *The Principle of Reason*, Trans. Reginald Lilly. Bloomington: Indiana University Press, 1991, pp.88-90.

3. Marshall McLuhan, Letter to Ezra Pound. This formulation became the tetrad; the model of laws with which to study media scientifically.

4. Sefer Yetzirah. In blue print as according to Kabbalistic thinking, the letters are the blueprint for the universe. According to Psalm 104, the letters of the Hebrew alphabet for the "creation" were used as the builder uses his actual bricks in the construction of his building.

5. And though it is called "the closing of the gates", the Ark (which contains the Scrolled Torah) remains open for the entire

service signifying that the gates of heaven are wide open to prayers and entreaties. And like Noah's Ark, the language of the Torah signifies a means of safety and escape. Arced like the airplane itself. Also transliterated through Hebrew, gate (get) means divorce—as we divorce ourselves through one plane of being into another.

6. For, according to the Zohar, all the letters fly up in the air, from that higher air, subtle and unknowable. They go up and come down.

7. See Sefer Yetzirah, *2:2*. Wesier Edition, Trans. Aryeh Kaplan, San Francisco, 1997.

8. Elliot R. Wolfson, *Heidegger and Kabbalah: Hidden Gnosis and the Path of Poiesis*, Indiana University Press, 20919, p.5.

9. Like how for Derrida, "I try and distinguish between what one calls the Future and 'l'avenir' [the 'to come']. The future is that which—tomorrow, later, next century—will be. There is a future which is predictable, programmed, scheduled, foreseeable. But there is a future, l'avenir (to come) which refers to someone who comes whose arrival is totally unexpected. For me, that is the real future. That which is totally unpredictable. The Other who comes without my being able to anticipate their arrival. So, if there is a real future, beyond the other known future, it is l'avenir in that it is the coming of the Other when I am completely unable to foresee their arrival." Like Benjamin's, "Jetztzeit" (now-time) outlined in his *Theses on the Philosophy of History*, a notion of time that is ripe with revolutionary possibility; time that has been detached from the continuum of history; poised, filled with energy, ready to leap into an ever-becoming future. Both speaking to the equiprimordiality of past, present, future.

10. How the Alef came to be the first letter of the alphabet comes from an old Talmudic tale that goes like this: When the Creator thought to create the world, all the letters of the alphabet came to Him in reverse order from last (Tav) to first

(Alef). The letter Tav entered first and said, "Master of the world! It is good, and also seemly of You, to create the world with me, with my properties. Use me first—as I stand in for (truth) EmeT (which ends with the letter Tav). And You are called truth, so it's befitting that you should begin the universe with me, the letter Tav. But The Creator answered: "You are beautiful and sincere, but do not merit the world that I conceived to be created by your properties, since you are destined to be marked on the foreheads of the truly faithful who fulfill all of Torah from Alef to Tav (from the first letter to the last), and perished because of you." Essentially highlighting the dangers of univisional Truth (which leads to death). And instead, chose to start the alphabet with Alef, which is silent and contains all the letters within it. And numerologically referencing number one, it stands as a symbol of all that is present non present, a oneness that embodies an ever-multiplying subjectivity.

11. Most airplanes have four door entrances / exits and two window exits (762, 737-100/200/300/500/600/700 + Airbus 318/319 jets), and tiny holes called "bleed holes" in the bottom of the middle pane of each window which releases moisture and balances pressure ;)

12. Yet also plein from Late Latin, plenarius as in a conference plenary—open to all. Though the term "air-plane" came into use in 1907, the earliest uses are British, the word caught on in American English, where it largely superseded earlier aeroplance (1873 in this sense and still common in British English). Lord Byron, speculating on future travel, used air-vessel (1822); and in 1865 aeromotive (based on locomotive) was used, also as air-boat (1870).

13. In 2017, the U.S government conducted an experiment to try to determine how effective TSA screenings actually are at detecting dangerous materials like weapons. They simulated the screening process and sent bags with "test items" (ie. weapons) through the traditional procedure used to process passengers.

And the result determined that 95% of the items were not detected. Thus, every day, thousands of people go through an unnecessarily complex process that doesn't do anything to protect air travellers and could lead to an untold number of weapons slipping through security. See "'Disturbing' Undercover Probe Found TSA Screenings Missing Many Test Weapons", Tom Costello and Phil Helsel, Nov. 8, 2017, *US News*.

14. And also, for Bataille: "The limit is only there to be overreached. Fear and horror are not the real and final reaction; on the contrary, they are a temptation to overstep the bounds." Georges Bataille, *Eroticism: Death and Sensuality*.

15. Marquis de Sade, *Justine: The Misfortunes of Virtue*, 1791. *Justine, Philosophy in the Bedroom, and Other Writings*. Compiled by Richard Seaver, Translated from French by Austryn Wainhouse, Grove press, New York, 1971.

16. For according to Bataille, "extreme seductiveness is at the boundary of horror." See *Visions of Excess* and *Story of the Eye*.

17. In French, déborder means excess, exuberance, profusion, overflow; pleine à déborder: full to overflowing.

18. According to Kabbalistic hermeneutics, not only is the gematria for airplane (matos) commensurate with "assir" (captive) and "arah" (to flee)—but also and "l'aymar"—to say. Read through a 13 th C. numerologic frame, the airplane further highlights that to speak is to flee; to fly into language, through planes of being.

19. Michel Foucault, *Discipline and Punish*. Also, "The gaze is alert everywhere" and "The panoptic mechanism arranges spatial unities that make it possible to see constantly and to recognize immediately." And as the letters traveling the space, with lateral [ ]visibility we become that compact mass, a locus of multiple exchanges.

20. ie open to hijacking, illegality, emigration, it's is always in a state of negotiation. See Derrida in "Autoimmunity"

"vulnerable spaces such as air[planes] are integral to the existence of democracy, in their very vulnerability". Rogues (Stanford: Stanford University Press, 2005).

21. Such as employing Pratt and Whitney or General Electric at the same time. Like with language itself, for an airplane, it's possible to gain altitude with 2 engines, but having two engines out on one side makes the airplane harder to control and causes more drag—ie. the importation of multiple engines resists stability and keeps it from going "straight".

22. Aerotically exposing its internal circuity, wing flaps regulate lift or drag.

23. Or more specifically, called emPENnage, derived from the French, empenner, to feather an arrow [aero], the structure at the rear of an aircraft that not only provides stability during flight but controls pitch.

24. Gilles Deleuze and Felix Guattari, *Anti Oedipus: Capitalism and Schizophrenia*. Minneapolis: University of Minnesota Press, 2000.

25. Like how language as a chordal concordance cuts across international codes, systems, boundaries, the Concorde supersonic jet co-developed by the British and the French, was the first airline company to be co-owned internationally. Taking its name from the word "concord" (from Middle English and Old French concorde, Latin concordia, from concors 'of one mind', and from con- 'together' + cor, cord- 'heart'; a coming together), it's very being is synecdochic of linguistic usage—how a concord refers to the agreement between parts of speech; "...a concord of sweet sounds..." William Shakespeare, *Merchant of Venice*, Act V, Scene I. Also, the Concorde was the only passenger plane to ever cross the sound barrier. And echoing Derrida, as outlined in "A Silkworm of One's Own," the Concord[e] houses truth as accord, a kinship of correspondences. [For I am weary, weary of the truth and of the truth as untruth of a being—

there, each time in the truth and the untruth uncovering and re-covering, unveiling and veiling dissimulation or withdrawal and non-withdrawal, weary of this opposition that is not an opposition as revelation a veiling]. *Veils*, Hélène Cixous and Jacques Derrida; trans. Geoffrey Bennington, Stanford University Press, California, 2001.

26. Excess, expenditure, sacrifice, ecstatic abandon as laid out in Georges Bataille's *La Notion de dèpense.*

27. This sense of limit is reminiscent of the Kabbalistic nation of Tzimtzum—how contraction is expansion; and infinite essence must be contained. Or, in the language of the Azriel of Gerona, the sefirotic potencies which collectively are the disclosure of the Tetragrammaton, are the limited force that is unlimited. In the words of Lauren Bacall in *To Have and Have Not:* "Just put your lips together and blow".

28. Or in Heideggerian terms (einklang). einklang klang klang goes the poly.

29. In some ways related to how Derrida writes in La carte postale: De Socrate à Freud et au-delà using the form of the private to inadvertently create something public—ie. as a mode of both public and private transportation, this is particularly noteworthy in that we literally become par avian, mailed through space and time. Jacques Derrida, *The Post Card: From Socrates to Freud and Beyond*, University of Chicago Press, Chicago, 1987.

30. Like language communicated by way of the internet, (armed with data and broken up into individual packets is, sent out and connects back at its destination where it unloads its "information"), claimed and reclaimed from both intended and unintended destinations, the airplane metonymically stands in for the infinite ways information gets transmitted.

 Adeena Karasick, Ph.D, is a New York based poet, performer, cultural theorist and media artist, author of 12 books of poetry and poetics. Her Kabbalistically inflected, urban, Jewish feminist mashups have been described as "electricity in language" (Nicole Brossard); "proto-ecstatic jet-propulsive word torsion" (George Quasha); noted for their "cross-fertilization of punning and knowing, theatre and theory" (Charles Bernstein); "a twined virtuosity of mind and ear which leaves the reader deliciously lost in Karasick's signature 'syllabic labyrinth'" (Craig Dworkin); "demonstrating how desire flows through language, an unstoppable flood of allusion (both literary and pop-cultural), word-play, and extravagant and outrageous sound-work." (Mark Scroggins). Most recently is *Massaging the Medium: 7 Pechakuchas*, (The Institute of General Semantics Press: 2022), shortlisted for Outstanding Book of the Year Award (ICA, 2023); *Checking In* (Talonbooks, 2018); and *Salomé: Woman of Valor* (University of Padova Press, Italy, 2017). The libretto for her Spoken Word opera, *Salomé: Woman of Valor* CD, (NuJu Records, 2020); and *Salomé Birangona*, translation into Bengali (Boibhashik Prokashoni Press, Kolkata, 2020). Karasick teaches Literature and Critical Theory for the Humanities and Media Studies Dept. at Pratt Institute, is Poetry Editor for *Explorations in Media Ecology,* Associate International Editor of *New Explorations: Studies in Culture and Communication*, 2021 Andrew W. Mellon Foundation Award recipient and winner of the Voce Donna Italia award for her contributions to feminist thinking, and has just been appointed Poet Laureate of the Institute of General Semantics. The "Adeena Karasick Archive" is established at Special Collections, Simon Fraser University.

Made in the USA
Middletown, DE
11 February 2024

49124662R00064